5-Minute Daily Practice

Writing

BY MARC TYLER NOBLEMAN

SCHOLASTIC
PROFESSIONAL BOOKS

New York • Toronto • London • Auckland • Sydney • Mexico City
New Delhi • Hong Kong • Buenos Aires

Cover design by **Gerard Fuchs**
Cover art by **Dave Clegg**
Interior design by **Holly Grundon**
Interior illustrations by **Mike Moran** and **Jared Lee**

ISBN: 0-439-26244-5
Copyright © 2003 by Marc Tyler Nobleman
All rights reserved. Published by Scholastic Inc.
Printed in the U.S.A.

4 5 6 7 8 9 10   40   09 08 07 06 05

Contents

Introduction

How can you help your students become better writers? One way is to provide them with inspiring prompts. This book makes it easy to do that. You'll find 180 prompts sure to spark your students' imaginations and make it simple for you to include writing as a part of the daily schedule.

The prompts in this book are designed to encourage students to try a wide variety of writing styles. There are expository, persuasive, descriptive, and narrative prompts. You'll also find one-sentence story starters and endings. A section of longer starters and endings gives your students a chance to use their critical-thinking skills to figure out how to complete the story.

How to Use These Activities

You may want to copy the shorter prompts onto the chalkboard. You could also copy each prompt onto an index card and invite students to choose a card each day. You may want to reproduce and cut apart the prompts on each page to give to students. Another alternative is to make an overhead transparency of each page. Leave all but the daily prompt covered each day.

Persuasive Prompts

Name: _____

1. Imagine your town is going to be renamed. What do you think its new name should be? Write a letter to the editor of your town newspaper making a case for your choice.

Persuasive Prompts

Name: _____

2. What is your favorite television show? Write a paragraph persuading your classmates to watch the show.

Persuasive Prompts

Name: _____

3. What kind of music do you like best? Hip-hop? Classical? Rock and roll? Write about your favorite and try to persuade others to your point of view.

Persuasive Prompts

Name: _____

4. Do you think your lunch period is long enough? How could you persuade your school to make it longer?

Persuasive Prompts

Name: _____

5. Do you think that weekends should be longer? In your answer, include persuasive reasons for extending weekends.

Persuasive Prompts

Name: _____

6. What picture book did you like best when you were younger? Write about it in a way that would convince kids in first grade to read it.

Persuasive Prompts

Name: _____

7. Some communities have a law banning skateboarding in public places. Do you agree or disagree with this law? Be sure to support your position.

Persuasive Prompts

Name: _____

8. Do you think a cat or a dog makes a better pet? Write a paragraph explaining your choice.

Persuasive Prompts

Name: _____

9. You have just heard about a well–paying babysitting job. Write a persuasive paragraph explaining why you would be an excellent choice for the job.

Persuasive Prompts

Name: _____

10. Your teacher said you could have a homework-free weekend if you give her a good reason for it. Write a speech that would convince her.

Name: _____

11. Make a list of five adjectives you could use to describe an ideal pet. Then use the words to write a description of this pet.

Name: _____

12. What's the worst movie you've seen this year? Write a review of it.

Name: _____

13. What's your favorite restaurant? Pretend you're a restaurant critic. Write a review of your favorite restaurant.

Name: _____

14. What qualities do you look for in a friend? Write a paragraph describing a good friend.

Name: _____

15. Describe the best birthday you've ever had.

Name: _____

16. Imagine an absolutely perfect day. Describe it.

Name: _____

17. Describe your very first friend. What was special about him or her?

Name: _____

18. Plan a surprise party for your best friend. Tell a story about how you would make sure he or she was surprised.

Name: _____

19. You just got a new puppy. You've only had it for an hour when you realize it can do something no other dog can do. Describe what it can do.

Name: _____

20. What is your dream job? Describe a day in your life while working at your dream job.

Name: _____

21. Do you like to do your homework at a desk in your room? At the kitchen table? Tell about where and how you like to do your homework.

Name: _____

22. What rules do you have in your classroom? List them and explain the reason for each rule.

Name: _____

23. What's your favorite sport? Write an explanation of the sport so someone who's never heard of it can understand how to play it.

Name: _____

24. You just won $50,000! Describe how you would use the money.

Name: _____

25. What's the most embarrassing thing that's ever happened to you? Write about it and explain why it was so embarrassing.

Name: _____

26. What holiday do you like the best? Explain what you do on that holiday and why you like it best.

Name: _____

27. Write directions for a friend explaining how to get from the school to your house.

Name: _____

28. There's a new student in your class from another country who's never had a peanut butter and jelly sandwich. Write step-by-step directions for the student explaining how to make one.

Name: _____

29. If you could meet any famous person, who would you choose? What questions would you ask? Write five questions you would ask.

Name: _____

30. How are you like your best friend? How are you different? Write a paragraph in which you compare and contrast yourself with your best friend.

Name: _____

31. Write a mysterious story with this title: "The Strange Case of Ms. Beenie's Disappearing Chalkboard."

Name: _____

32. You find a magic stone on your way home from school. When you rub the stone, magical things happen. Tell a story about what happens to you.

Name: _____

33. Your aunt arrives with a huge box. You hear strange noises coming from the box. Write a story about what's inside.

Name: _____

34. You arrive at school one day and suddenly realize you're invisible to your teacher and your classmates. Describe what happens to you that day.

Narrative

Name: _____

35. Although you asked for an MP3 player for your birthday, your parents gave you a telescope. But it's not just any telescope. Something amazing happens when you look through it. Tell a story about what happens when you use the telescope.

Name: _____

36. It rains on the day of your class picnic. The class can't play any of the outdoor games they had planned. But the picnic is more fun than ever! Write a story explaining why it's so much fun.

Name: _____

37. One day you wake up and discover your family has acquired a robot helper! Tell a story about how the robot changes your family's life.

Narrative Prompts

Name: _____

38. You win $200 in a contest! Write a story about how you use the money.

Narrative Prompts

Name: _____

39. Choose one character, one setting, and one plot from the choices below, and then use your choices to tell a story.

Character	Setting	Plot
• a dinosaur	• New York City	• has trouble making friends
• an athletic princess	• a deserted island	• is lost
• a famous racecar driver	• outer space	• is being chased by an evil turtle

Narrative Prompts

Name: _____

40. Your time machine has taken you 500 years into the future. Write a story about what life is like at this future time.

Life's Most Embarrassing Moments

Starter

Name: _____

41. Forgetting My Own Birthday

I have a great memory. I know all the presidents of the United States, in order. I could tell you the first and last names of all the kids in my school. I never forget the birthday of anybody in my family. That's why it's so hard to believe that one year, I actually forgot my own birthday!

At breakfast that day, my parents were acting a little weird. They probably thought I was the one acting weird because I didn't mention my birthday. I didn't know their big birthday surprise for me would happen after school.

When I walked into my classroom, there were birthday decorations everywhere. My friends were ready to celebrate. Still, I didn't think it was all for me. Finally, I realized it was my birthday when . . .

Life's Most Embarrassing Moments

Ending

Name: _____

42. Slipping in the Cafeteria

. . . and that's when I lost my balance.

Luckily, I landed on my backside and wasn't hurt. Meanwhile, my lunch tray hit the ground loudly and food splattered everywhere. That was the noise that made everyone turn around and look at me. I turned bright red with embarrassment.

My friends came to help me up. Seth couldn't resist saying "I told you not to do that! If you'd listened to me, you never would have slipped."

Name: _____

Ending

43. Missing the Ball

. . . I was having a great game until that happened. In fact, I don't remember our team ever having played so well, which only made me more frustrated.

The worst part about it was that there were only minutes left when I made that mistake. And boy, was it a big one!

However, my teammates were nice about it. Andrew said, "We're not mad at you."

Cassie said, "It's okay. We all miss the ball sometimes."

"Yeah," said Justin, "but none of us have ever done it in such a funny way!"

Name: _____

Starter

44. Secret Crush

I was the only person who knew I had a secret crush on Chris, or so I thought. Chris was new in school and very nice.

Imagine my shock when I found a note on the classroom floor that read "Guess who likes Chris?" And there, underneath in big letters, was my name!

Who wrote that? I wondered. *And how many people saw it?* I started to worry that a lot of people knew about my crush on Chris.

Luckily, everyone was on the playground when I found the note, so I could get rid of it before anyone else could see it. I turned to throw it out, and standing right in front of me was . . .

Name: _____

Ending

45. Milk Shot out of My Nose

. . . several more kids came into the principal's office. I was
even more embarrassed now, but I also wanted to laugh.

Kevin's shirt was covered with tomato sauce, and Mike's
pants were splattered with something brown—maybe gravy?
Clumps of mashed potatoes were in Rachel's hair, and I thought
I saw a piece or two of ravioli in Randi's.

I couldn't believe it had all started over a little carton of milk.

Name: _____

Ending

46. Thanksgiving in Dimension Z

. . . which is why, twice a year, the Zites (the inhabitants of Dimension Z)
get together with their families and give thanks. They all wear the traditional
Thanksgiving outfit, inspired by the very first Zite Thanksgiving thousands of
years ago. And they each eat two delicious servings of opbort, also a very old
Thanksgiving custom in Dimension Z.

They are proud because Dimension Z is the only place that celebrates
Thanksgiving twice a year, and now you know why!

Name: _____

Starter

47. Independence Day on Weird World

Americans celebrate Independence Day every Fourth of July. It's a festive time when we remember how hard our ancestors fought for the freedom to run the new country themselves. The creatures on Weird World also celebrate Independence Day, but not in July—they don't even have a month called July! Their Independence Day isn't about freedom from another country, it's about . . .

Name: _____

Ending

48. Family Day in the Zigzag Zone

. . . just like they do every year on Family Day. When that's done, the family climbs into its crooked car together to begin the day's final—and most exciting—annual event: the Zigzag Race. As you probably guessed, the race must be done in a zigzag (like everything else in the Zigzag Zone).

Family Day is a time to be together, whether you prefer moving in a straight line or a crooked one!

Name: _____

49. Halloween on Chura 5114

The first day of the new year on Chura 5114 is Halloween. Churians always expect to hear the first knock at the door around 5 A.M., when the first treat-or-trickers usually show up, hoping to get some great vegetables tossed in their sack. On Chura 5114, the kids don't go out on Halloween—the adults do! (But the kids are always very excited because the adults come back and share all the vegetables with them.)

This year, the most popular Halloween costume was a "Human Being," a creature from a planet called Earth in the Milky Way galaxy. Until recently, most Churians didn't know what a human being was. They learned about humans last year when . . .

Name: _____

50. Memorial Day in the Land of Ug

. . . agreed to hold a meeting. The Ug Council needed to discuss what to do to honor the memory of the brave Uggers who participated in the heroic act that saved their land.

It didn't take long for the Council to decide that they should create a holiday to pay tribute to them. The day they chose to celebrate the holiday was the day when the Uggers first gathered to protect their people.

Now every Memorial Day in the Land of Ug, colorful flags are flown and the names of all the heroes of Ug are printed on the front page of every newspaper.

Alternate Universe Holidays

Name: _____

Starter

51. Mother's Day on Asteroid Amam

One asteroid that contains life in the Andreae galaxy is called Amam. Mother's Day on Amam is very unique because the date changes every year. One year you might celebrate on November 28, and the next on March 14 or July 8. That way, the Mother's Day gifts are not the only surprises—Mother's Day is, too!

This year, sister and brother Siri and Woron chose January 2 for Mother's Day. As always, they woke their mom up first thing in the morning—to Amamians, that happens to be in the middle of the night! Then, they began with their favorite Mother's Day custom of . . .

Wacky Interviews

Name: _____

Ending

52. Oldest Person

Interviewer: Wow, that's old. I don't think anybody will believe it!

World's Oldest Person: They can look at my birth certificate! It's written by hand.

Interviewer: Any final words of advice for the rest of us?

World's Oldest Person: If you do all of the things to stay young and fit that I just told you about, some of you might even beat my record someday.

Name: _____

Wacky Interviews

Starter

53. Fastest Runner

Interviewer: The world's fastest runner doesn't slow down very much, so we're lucky today to get this interview.

World's Fastest Runner: It's my pleasure.

Interviewer: How fast can you run?

World's Fastest Runner: Faster than a turtle but slower than a cheetah.

Interviewer: So you're actually the world's fastest human runner.

World's Fastest Runner: Yes, but that doesn't sound as good.

Interviewer: When did you realize you were so fast?

World's Fastest Runner: I don't remember this, of course, but my parents tell me that it was right after I was born. When I was only a few weeks old, they noticed that I . . .

Name: _____

Wacky Interviews

Ending

54. Bravest Person

Interviewer: Were you scared when it happened?

World's Bravest Person: Yes, I was, but I didn't let my fear get to me.

Interviewer: That shows that you truly deserve the title "World's Bravest Person."

World's Bravest Person: Thank you, but I've seen many brave people. I'm only one of them.

Interviewer: Still, what you did that day was remarkable. It took amazing courage. I'm sure it will be very inspiring to everyone reading this.

Name: _____

Starter

55. Smartest Child

Interviewer: Everyone knows that kids are very smart, and today I'm here to talk with a kid who has been called the world's smartest. Just how smart are you?

World's Smartest Child: Smart enough to know that I don't believe that title! I'm flattered, but there are so many smart kids in the world. How could anyone compare us all?

Interviewer: Why did people start calling you the "World's Smartest Child"?

World's Smartest Child: Probably because I learned to do math at a very young age. I learned to read when I was even younger.

Interviewer: What was the first book you read, and how old were you?

World's Smartest Child: Believe it or not, the first book I read was . . .

Name: _____

Starter

56. Tenochtitlán (Mexico)

Being an Aztec emperor was amazing. He wore gold sandals. Every time he took a step, nobles swept the floor in front of him, and covered the ground with beautiful cloth. Even still, the emperor rarely walked anywhere—he was carried, lounging on a litter. No one was allowed to look at his face or turn his or her back on him. Even family members had to leave the room backward. One day, the emperor was being carried around on his litter, when . . .

Weird History

Name: _____

Ending

57. Stonehenge (England)

. . . then the pair of renowned archeologists turned and walked slowly away from Stonehenge.

Seth said, "Wow, we came to Stonehenge to study the ancient monument, but I never dreamed we would see what we saw today. People usually think of rocks when they think of Stonehenge, but that was definitely not a rock."

Dara said, "Stonehenge is a mysterious place. There are still many questions about it. Who put these huge stones here in the middle of a grassy plain in England thousands of years ago? And how were those ancient people able to move the stones without trucks?"

"I think what we saw today might be a clue to help us answer those questions," Seth said smiling.

Weird History

Name: _____

Starter

58. Easter Island (off the coast of Chile)

Maxine is an amateur petrologist, meaning a person who studies rocks. She was very excited to take a trip to the island of Rapa Nui. We know it as Easter Island, which is what Europeans called it after landing there in 1722. It is a remote spot, over 2,000 miles west of Chile. The island is famous for its large stone statues shaped like heads.

Those heads are exactly what Maxine wanted to see. She wanted to examine the statues up close. That's where Maxine was when she tripped on something shiny that was sticking out of the hillside. As she bent down to pick it up, a person who lived on the island ran over to her.

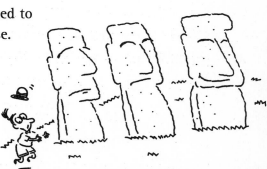

"Please, don't touch that!" he said. "It's . . ."

Name: _____

Weird History

Ending

59. Colosseum (Rome, Italy)

. . . but the renowned archaeologists Seth and Dara figured something unusual like that would happen during their visit to Rome's Colosseum. After all, this magnificent structure has a very shocking history. They just never expected a piece of that history to fall and clunk Seth right on the head!

The Colosseum is a giant, circular arena built in the first century C.E. A big piece of its outer wall is missing. Today, it is a tourist attraction, but when it was new, it was often used for epic contests between wild animals and gladiators. Thousands of people attended. They were even able to fill up the Colosseum with water to have battles between real ships!

Seth and Dara were eager to show their friends the photograph of the piece that fell on them. Hopefully the museum's curator would know exactly what it was a piece of, because they sure didn't.

Name: _____

Weird History

Starter

60. Machu Picchu (Peru)

There is a mystery high above Peru in the Andes mountains. It's a city called Machu Picchu that was "lost" for hundreds of years. The Incans built it sometime before 1500 to defend themselves against the Spaniards. No one is sure why or when the city was abandoned, but it remained hidden for several centuries.

The archaeologist Hy Dan Seeke was studying Machu Picchu when he discovered a secret chamber in one of the religious temples. As he opened the ancient door, sunlight flooded the room for the first time in many centuries. His eyes widened when he saw . . .

Name: _____

Weird History

Ending

61. Pompeii (Italy)

". . . which is why this is such an important discovery!" Dara told Seth, showing him what she was holding.

It was very typical that Seth and Dara, the renowned archeologists, would find something so interesting during their first visit to Pompeii, the famous city that was buried by the volcanic eruption of Mount Vesuvius in 79 C.E.

"I think it's important, too," Seth said. "Many people know that Pompeii was destroyed when the volcano erupted, but there are still mysteries here. Like this."

Dara said, "People have explored these ruins for centuries and have uncovered all sorts of things—even buildings—that are still perfectly preserved under the volcano's ash. It's amazing! But I don't think anyone has found anything as beautiful as what we found here today."

Name: _____

On the Job With a . . .

Ending

62. Secret Agent

". . . this is exactly why I don't like to take anyone along on my top-secret missions!" the secret agent told me.

"I'm so sorry, Agent Tudor!" I said. "It was an accident!"

Agent Tudor appreciated the apology, but it didn't change the fact that we were stuck in the middle of nowhere without a phone, food, or a plan. Plus nobody else knew where we were, and a storm was coming.

We did manage to get out of our predicament, but believe it or not, that story is not nearly as interesting as how we got into the predicament in the first place.

Name: _____

On the Job With a . . .

Starter

63. Matador

On my first trip to Spain I met a real matador! Maria is one of the world's first female matadors. She happened to be sitting in the lobby of my hotel, and the desk clerk told me who she was. I was very nervous to go up to her, but the clerk said it was okay.

I told her that I was from the United States and knew nothing about bullfighting. Maria told me how scary it was at first because bulls are big and can be dangerous. However, as she practiced, she got more and more comfortable around them. Although many people are against the sport because animals get killed and people get hurt, it is a great honor to be a matador in Spain.

I asked Maria if she ever got hurt bullfighting. At first she said no, but then she admitted that her first day on the job did not go well. Something very interesting happened. As soon as she stepped into the ring . . .

Name: _____

On the Job With a . . .

Ending

64. Cartoonist

" . . . but I never in a million years expected to win. I only entered the cartoon contest because I was curious about the 'mystery prize.'"

"You must have been so excited when they announced that you were the winner," the cartoonist said.

"I was totally surprised," I said. "I've thought back over the last few months— where I first saw the contest advertised, who convinced me to enter, and what I drew. And after all that, I actually won!"

"Well, I'm glad you did, because I enjoyed showing you my studio and how I work."

"It was even more fun for me. I thought the mystery prize would be a gift certificate or something like that. Spending time with a famous cartoonist was much better! And the best part of all is that you weren't the only part of the mystery prize. My friends will never believe what else I got!"

Name: _____

65. Rocket Scientist

My school bus drove by the space lab every day, and I always wanted to visit. My friend's father knew a scientist there named Mr. Sapper. I wrote him an e-mail asking if I could see the lab sometime. Minutes later, Mr. Sapper wrote back: "Yes!"

The night before my visit, I couldn't sleep. I stared out the window at the stars.

I got the feeling that the stars were alive. There must be more than twinkling lights out there! I didn't want to ask Mr. Sapper what he thought. He might think I'm crazy.

At the lab, everything looked so complicated. While Mr. Sapper explained how they figured out how to build the rockets I couldn't help but think about the stars I saw the night before. I decided to ask him if he thought there were other living things somewhere else in the universe.

"Good question. I used to think not, but since I started working here . . ."

Name: _____

66. Dinosaur Fossil Hunter

. . . which was the last place I would have thought to look for dinosaur bones.

After a long, hot day of digging without luck, I'm glad Debbie tried one more spot. Debbie was the best paleontologist I'd ever met. Then again, she was the only one that I'd ever met. How often do you meet a person who learns about prehistoric life by studying fossils? Not often. When she visited our school, I told her that I'd like to come along sometime, but I never thought she'd say yes.

"Finally, we found one!" she said. I could only see a little bit of the bone in the ground, as Debbie dusted off the top. She was very happy.

"It looks like a big one," I said.

"Actually, it's quite small," she said. That made me wonder what a big one looked like!

When we found that bone, it made me better understand all the stories Debbie had told me that day.

Name: _____

On the Job With a . . .

Starter

67. Skyscraper Window Washer

My mom works on the top floor of an office building that is 40 stories high. That's 38 stories higher than our house, so you can tell I'm not used to heights.

On the first day of summer vacation, I came to work with her. I was sitting in an empty office down the hall from my mom's office, reading a book. Suddenly, I heard a tapping behind me.

I turned to see a window washer smiling at me! The only time I'd ever really seen one was from the ground. He waved and pointed down. I didn't want to look. When he did it again, I realized he was telling me to go down one floor. I asked my mom if I could go, and she said it was okay. She knew him and told me that he was a nice guy named Darren.

I took the elevator down to the 39th floor and rushed to the window. Darren was there! It was amazing. He gestured for me to open a window.

"The windows on the top floor don't open," Darren said. "Sorry I made you come down here."

"That's okay," I said.

"Want to know the weirdest thing I ever saw while washing windows way up here?" he asked.

I nodded.

He said, "I was outside the 62nd floor of another building when I noticed . . ."

Name: _____

Ending

68. Leprechaun

. . . but we were a long way from Ireland, where leprechauns supposedly live.

"That's a great story, but I still don't believe in leprechauns."

"Did you see that?" Leslie asked.

"I don't know what I saw," Dan said.

"It couldn't have been a real leprechaun," Diana said. "Leprechauns aren't real."

There are many small, green things in the forest, but how many of them wear little hats? All four of us swore we saw something wearing a little hat as it jumped from the branch to the path and scurried away, faster than a squirrel.

Even the smallest things can turn an ordinary morning hike into a mystery. We still don't know what we saw, but we always tell the story because we want to believe that we really saw a leprechaun.

Name: _____

Starter

69. Loch Ness Monster

Most kids would love to have relatives in Scotland. That's where Loch Ness is—and where Loch Ness is, some say that's where a monster is, too!

Of course, I don't believe in the Loch Ness Monster . . . anyway, I didn't use to.

Two nights ago, I begged my aunt and uncle to take me to the lake again. ("Loch" is Scottish for "lake.") They'd taken me before but we never saw anything.

The lake is huge. We stopped the car and walked closer. I scanned the water with my binoculars but didn't see any movement. After a few minutes, I gave up.

As we walked back to the car, we heard a splashing sound. I whipped around and quickly looked through my binoculars. That's when I saw . . .

Name: _____

Did You See That?

Ending

70. Ghost

. . . and that's why we ran for our lives! Well, that might be an exaggeration, but we sure were scared. Nobody looked back until we got to the front porch, and when we looked then, it was gone.

All three of us went inside and immediately looked in the book that the strange, old man had given us earlier.

"Did you see that?" Rachel said.

"We never should have gone in that cave," Julie said.

"But that's why we went out there! We wanted to see if it really exists," Rachel said.

Flipping through the pages, we found the right picture.

"Yes, that's it. That's what it was," Julie said.

"I like it much better on paper than in person," I said.

Name: _____

Did You See That?

Starter

71. Alien

A humming noise woke me up. When I looked out my second-floor bedroom window, the noise suddenly stopped. Nobody was out mowing any lawns.

Then the humming noise started again, and I looked up at the sky. A flying saucer was hovering over my house. Maybe I should say it this way: "A FLYING SAUCER WAS HOVERING OVER MY HOUSE!"

"Did you see that?" I said. Then I realized I was talking to myself. Nobody else was around.

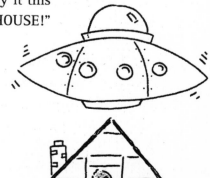

An odd-looking ladder lowered from the bottom of the flying saucer. But, somehow I wasn't scared. The flying saucer looked very peaceful.

A creature began climbing down the ladder. As it got closer, I noticed . . .

Name: _____

72. Bigfoot

I used to dislike going to camp, but not because I was afraid of Bigfoot. (It was because I was afraid of snakes.)

Now I love camping, and it's all because of Bigfoot! What happened?

At summer camp, we'd stay in cabins. It wasn't really "roughing it," but it was still very different from living in a house or an apartment.

Sometimes, we'd hear things outside the cabin at night. Usually, it was the wind blowing through the trees. But one night, we thought we heard an animal.

My friends and I wanted to see what kind of animal might be making the noise, so we crept outside. At first, we didn't see anything but soon we saw a snake nearby! There were five of us and only one snake, but I was still nervous.

The snake slithered under some leaves.

"Did you see that?" Ian said. "That snake was huge!"

Elliot said, "But it couldn't have made that noise we heard."

Before we moved a muscle, something even more huge than the snake came out of the woods, looked at us, and . . .

Name: _____

73. Superhero

. . . that was when everyone looked up in the sky. Sure enough, there was something flying very fast overhead, something—someone—wearing a bright green cape.

"Did you see that?" someone in the crowd said.

"I don't believe my own eyes," someone else said. "But if you saw it, then I guess I saw it, too."

I smiled because I knew who it was. I'm the only one who knew the truth about my city's new superhero.

Name: _____

74. In a Movie Line

My parents surprised my sister and me on the first day of summer vacation. We went to see the big, new movie starring my favorite actor—on opening night!

In line at the cinema, my sister was telling us about the party her class had on the last day of school. She stopped for a moment, trying to remember the name of one of the games they'd played.

That's when I overheard the person in front of us say to his friend, "You must be so excited because this is the first movie you've ever seen."

His friend looked older than our parents! How could this be his first movie? The only reason I could think of was . . .

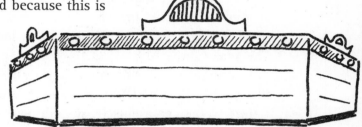

Name: _____

75. Under a Tree House

Jason and I were still standing under the tree house, and Jason's brother Joel was still up there, so we had to be quiet. We didn't want Joel to know we were there.

"No," I whispered, "I'm positive I heard it right. Joel definitely said, 'Jason doesn't know that he has a twin.'"

"But I don't have a twin!" Jason said in a loud whisper. "My only brother is Joel."

"I think the only way to find out the truth is to climb up there right now and ask him," I said.

Jason didn't like that idea at first, but he was so curious that he finally agreed to do it. Imagine how surprised he was when he saw . . .

Name: _____

Starter

76. In a Hotel Elevator

I was eight years old when I first went into an elevator. Since I lived in a small town, the buildings were only a few stories tall and didn't have elevators. But my family was on vacation in New York City, where it seems like every building has them!

After a long day of sightseeing, my parents were very tired. They plopped on the bed to rest.

"Let's call room service for a snack," my mom said.

"May I go downstairs to get it instead?" I asked. I wanted to ride the elevator as much as possible.

My parents said okay. The building had 40 floors and we were on the 32nd. If there were a lot of people in the elevator, it could be a long ride down.

But there were only two women in the elevator, and they were both hotel employees. We all smiled and said, "hi," then I started watching the numbers drop lower and lower.

One of the women said, "Now you'll believe me when you hear about the elephant on the 40th floor." The other woman laughed.

I couldn't believe what I'd just heard! As soon as we got to the lobby, I pretended to exit the elevator, but then I got right back in and pressed the button for the 40th floor.

When the doors opened on the top floor, the first thing I saw was . . .

Name: _____

Overheard the Strangest Thing

Starter

77. On the Beach

". . . the snow was up to my knees on this beach."

It was the hottest day of the year when my friend Gabriela and I overheard that. The sand was so hot, our bare feet could hardly stand it.

"Did she say what I think she said?" I asked Gabriela. "Did she say that just yesterday, the snow was up to her knees on this beach?"

We turned around to look at the man and woman we had just passed. They were in bathing suits, lying on a towel. People all around us were swimming, playing ball, and building sand castles.

"That's what I heard," Gabriela said. "But I just remembered something. Here's why I think she said that . . ."

Name: _____

Overheard the Strangest Thing

Ending

78. At the Zoo

. . . and that's when it came charging right at us! Then it stopped, but we knew it would.

So that's what the zookeeper meant when we overheard him tell a tour group not to take photographs.

My friend Lee said, "I'm so glad there's a cage between that animal and us."

"One thing is for sure," I said. "If there wasn't, we'd be running right now."

Name: _____

Starter

79. In the Principal's Office

I was sitting in the principal's office, but it's not what you're thinking. I wasn't sent there because of bad behavior. I was there to interview our principal, Mr. Whitfield, for a school project.

We were supposed to meet at 11 A.M., but it was already 11:10. Mr. Whitfield was usually very punctual, so I figured there had to be a good reason that he was late.

At 11:15, his assistant, Ms. Konareski, peeked into his office and then came over to me. "He should be right with you," she said. "He's just finishing up another meeting."

At 11:20, Mr. Whitfield and another man I've never seen before came out of his office, walking quickly into a meeting room. All I heard was the other man say, "If your idea works, then lunch and recess will become the students' least favorite parts of the school day!"

Suddenly, Mr. Whitfield popped back out and came over to me. "Sorry I've kept you waiting," he said politely. "I promise I'll be ready by 11:30. Is that okay?"

"Sure," I said. He thanked me and rushed back into the meeting room.

That gave me ten more minutes to try to figure out what they were talking about. My best guess was . . .

Name: _____

Ending

80. The Day We Got Electricity

. . . that's why they didn't think it would work. Like a lot of other people in 1900, my great-grandpa Frank was used to reading by gaslight.

"For hundreds of years—thousands even—people read by the light of a fire, and I don't see why that should change now!" he said.

My great-grandma Bertha said, "If you feel that way, maybe we should move out of our house. Our ancestors lived in caves." Then she giggled.

Grandpa Frank tried not to laugh, but he couldn't help it. "You're right. Let's take a look at this thing again," he said, taking something out of a bag. He held it up to Grandma Bertha.

"It's called a light bulb," he said.

Name: _____

Starter

81. When This Was a Dirt Road

The main road in my city is six lanes wide. It was about the same width one hundred years ago, only then it was made of dirt instead of asphalt.

When my mom was a little girl, her grandmother Ethel (my great-grandmother) used to walk down the road with her. It wasn't dirt anymore, but it wasn't crowded with shops and restaurants yet, either.

Ethel used to say, "When it rained, oh, what an awful mess! The whole street turned to mud."

"Yuck!" my mom would say.

"But people still needed to get places, so they'd walk in the mud and show up totally dirty. In fact, one time it rained so hard that . . ."

Name: _____

Ending

82. Old-Time Blizzard

. . . and that was my favorite part of the story.

Whenever it snowed, my grandmother would tell me this story about the worst blizzard she ever experienced.

"Did the newspaper say there was going to be such a big storm?" I asked her.

"No, it was a big surprise to everyone," she said.

As I looked at the snowflakes piling up on our windowsill, I thought about how amazing it must have been for my grandmother and her family to have experienced that much snow.

Name: _____

Ending

83. House Call

". . . but after all that, it was nothing serious," my grandma said. "Just a little cold."

"Grandma!" I said. "The doctor came over for a cold?"

"It was a different time back then. I liked him a lot because he always brought me a surprise—like a piece of chocolate."

"And that was the last time Dr. Neuman came to your house?" I asked.

"I believe so," she said. "Soon after that, doctors stopped making house calls. People started going to hospitals more."

"Wow," I said. "The doctors must have been sad. It sounds fun to visit people all day and make them feel better."

My grandma said, "It was always nice to see the doctor, even when nobody was sick."

Starter

Name: _____

84. Meeting the President

At least once a year, my dad would hear a certain story from his dad. Now I hear that same story at least once a year from my dad! It's a great story.

When my granddad was a little boy, his dad (my great-granddad) took him to the big city. Neither of them had ever been to any big city before, so it was quite a treat to visit Washington, D.C.

The first site they wanted to see was the White House. They didn't know what the White House looked like until they got there because they had never seen a picture of it in the newspaper, which was one of the only ways people got information back then.

Most people didn't have cameras in those days, so my great-granddad drew a picture of the White House, which my dad still has.

"Do you think we'll get to see President Roosevelt?" my granddad asked.

"I would guess not," my great-granddad said. "Too hot out for the President to be walking about, don't you think?"

"No, I don't think so," my granddad said. "I think it's perfect out."

"I agree with the young man," a voice behind them said. They turned and saw . . .

5-Minute Daily Practice: Writing   Scholastic Professional Books

Name: _____

Starter

85. Landing at Ellis Island

"Everyone was so excited to go to America, to learn to speak English and, most of all, to see the Statue of Liberty! That was the biggest thrill for my parents—your great-grandparents," my grandpa said.

"Did it look the same as it does now?" I asked.

"Basically the same. Maybe a little shinier," he said.

"But you don't remember coming in on the boat, do you?" I asked.

"Heavens, no! I wasn't even born yet! This is a story that my parents used to tell me when I was very little."

"So what happened next?"

"The boat docked at Ellis Island in New York Harbor. That was where many immigrants landed in America."

"What did people do when they got off the boat?" I asked.

"Everyone had to be registered first, but my parents were young and excited. There was something they wanted to do before that," grandpa said. "They weren't supposed to, but they snuck out of line to go see . . ."

Name: _____

The Number One Rule

Starter

86. Wipe Your Feet

For months, my parents planned a big party to celebrate their wedding anniversary. It rained a lot on the day of the party, but I had to go out with my dad to buy food for the guests.

We got back and wiped our feet thoroughly. This was an important rule at our house. Mom was upstairs getting ready. We put the groceries down, and I went to see if she needed any help.

That's when I saw them. Muddy footprints. Dog prints! Somehow our dog, Scruples, must have gotten out and come back in without wiping his paws! I had to clean the pawprints up quickly before anyone arrived.

I followed the pawprints through the hall and into the living room. Just then, the doorbell rang. The first guests had arrived! And the living room was completely . . .

Name: _____

The Number One Rule

Ending

87. No Running in the House

. . . tripped and knocked it over! As I watched, it seemed to fall in slow motion. The brand-new, delicate gift we had just given mom hit the ground. It made a loud noise and shattered into a million pieces, or at least a thousand. My sister Darby laughed, but I sure didn't.

"Oh, no!" I said. "Please don't laugh. I'm in so much trouble!"

"You knew mom's rule," Darby said.

She was right. Mom's words kept running through my head: "No running in the house." A few months ago, that rule became very important in our house because I broke something else as I was rushing to answer the phone.

And this time, my reason for running wasn't even that good.

Name: _____

The Number One Rule

Starter

88. Put Your Bike Away

My friends and I always seem to be in a hurry. A lot of times, we'll ride our bikes right up to the front step of my house, jump off, and run inside.

My dad didn't like that, and I understand why. It could be dangerous, both for me and for everyone else. Somebody could trip on the bike. Luckily, no one ever did, but something else happened that made me pay attention to our number one rule: "Always put your bike away."

I came straight home after school for a quick snack. I grabbed a banana and headed back outside. I'd only been away from my bike for a minute, but . . .

Name: _____

The Number One Rule

Ending

89. Clean Your Room

. . . it was under a jacket that was lying on the floor in the messiest corner of my room. But it was too late.

I turned to my dad who was still standing in the doorway. "I found it, Dad," I said sadly.

"Which pile was it in?" he said, smiling a little bit.

"I know what you're thinking," I said. "This never would've happened if I kept my room clean."

My dad kidded around with me. "You know, that just might work!"

I called my friend to apologize, but I was still happy that I finally found it. It's very important to her. She was understanding, but disappointed because she really needed it that day, and I didn't find it in time.

At that moment, I made my own number one rule: "Always clean your room!" And I never broke that rule again.

Name: _____

The Number One Rule

Ending

90. Write Down Phone Messages

". . . he never showed up!" my dad said. "I drove all the way there, but Steve never showed up. I'd been looking forward to meeting him all week."

I thought about how excited my dad had been to meet Steve, and why.

"I don't believe it!" my mom said. "He didn't even call to let you know he couldn't make it."

That's the part that made me want to leave the room. My dad and mom didn't know that Steve actually did call, but my dad never got the message. Oops . . . I had to be honest, otherwise my dad would be angry with Steve. Steve didn't do anything wrong. I did.

"Uh, Dad," I said. "Remember the other day, when I had a lot of homework?"

"Yes . . . ," he said.

"I was so busy that I . . . well, Steve actually *did* call a few days ago, and I *did* write it down . . . only I forgot to give it to you."

I'm sure you can guess my dad's reaction, and this is, of course, why the number one rule at our house now is: "WRITE DOWN ALL PHONE MESSAGES—AND DELIVER THEM."

Name: _____

The Number One Rule

Starter

91. Don't Shout Across the House

My parents' bedroom is on the opposite side of our house from my bedroom. We communicate with each other in many ways. Sometimes I walk over to their side. Sometimes I call them on their cell phone. We've even used e-mail to communicate across the house!

One thing we don't and won't do anymore is shout, and this is why.

Last month, I was working on a school project in my room. I had a question that I knew my mom would know the answer to, but I didn't feel like going downstairs and walking all the way to her room. (It only takes a minute but I was feeling lazy.)

So I called to her. "Mom! Mom!" I yelled.

She didn't answer so I raised my voice even louder.

"MOM! I HAVE A QUESTION!"

I didn't hear any response from her, but I got a sense that she was angry. I don't know how, I just did. So I ended up walking downstairs to find her, and I was right. She was very mad because while I was screaming, she was trying to . . .

Name: _____

Dream Jobs

Starter

92. Asking a Doctor

Interviewer: I'm here with Dr. Denise Dimauro to ask her, "Besides your current job, what is your dream job?"

Doctor: Without question, being a doctor is my dream job, but my second choice would probably be a scuba diving instructor.

Interviewer: Interesting. That's quite different from a doctor!

Doctor: Right now, it's just a hobby, but I think I might like spending more time under the ocean's waves.

Interviewer: How long have you been interested in being a scuba diving instructor, and why?

Doctor: Ever since I was a little girl, I have . . .

Name: _____

Dream Jobs

Ending

93. Asking a Teacher

Interviewer: Wow, you've sure had a lot of jobs before becoming a teacher!

Teacher: Yes, and I liked them all, but none of them were my dream job.

Interviewer: I never would have guessed your dream job even if I tried a hundred times.

Teacher: If you think about it, it's not that different than what a teacher does. It's also a job that helps people.

Interviewer: That's true. But you'd have to move pretty far from your home here in Miami, Florida, to do it!

Name: _____

Dream Jobs

94. Asking an Astronaut

Starter

Interviewer: This is Christian Stockstone, an astronaut who has made 12 trips into space. An astronaut is a dream job for a lot of people.

Astronaut: It's a great job. You see things very few people ever get to see, such as the beauty of our planet from a distance.

Interviewer: Do you have a dream job, Christian? Besides being an astronaut, that is?

Astronaut: Let's see if you can guess. I'll give you a clue. I first thought about my dream job while I was orbiting Earth in outer space.

Interviewer: Uh, a photographer?

Astronaut: Good guess, but no.

Interviewer: Orbiting the Earth . . . hmm . . . something to do with the environment?

Astronaut: You're getting closer . . .

Interviewer: I've got it! A . . .

Name: _____

Dream Jobs

95. Asking a Police Officer

Ending

Interviewer: That dream job seems even more dangerous than being a police officer!

Officer: Maybe, maybe not. If you're careful, things aren't so dangerous, and I'm always very careful. I feel like I'm prepared for almost every situation.

Interviewer: Sometimes officers like you have to stay up all night. What would the hours be in your dream job?

Officer: I think they would be similar. But time flies when you're having fun, and I'd have a lot of fun doing that job. Anyway, I love being a police officer so much that I'll probably never change jobs.

Name: _____

Dream Jobs

Starter

96. Asking a Fishing Boat Captain

Interviewer: The waves are rough out here today, but it's worth it to speak with an actual fishing boat captain! I'm very interested in your real job, but you know that the Question of the Day is "What is your dream job?"

Captain: Believe it or not, my dream job also involves animals of the sea, but in a different way. I'd love to raise and train them at a place like Oceanville.

Interviewer: The famous family theme park?

Captain: Exactly. I'd love to get close to the killer whales and bark with the seals!

Interviewer: You get to see some of those animals in their natural environment. How do you feel when you see them in captivity?

Captain: That's why it would be my dream job. I would love to make sure that these animals . . .

Name: _____

Dream Jobs

Ending

97. Asking a Chef

Chef: To me, that job is just as delicious as being a chef!

Interviewer: And not as much pressure.

Chef: Right! As a chef, I'm hoping everyone will like my cooking. But as a restaurant critic, everyone would be hoping that I'd like *their* cooking!

Interviewer: The story about how you chose to be a chef instead of a critic is very interesting. What do you think would've happened if you didn't meet that chef when you were a young child?

Chef: Who knows? Maybe I would've been a doctor.

Starters and Endings

Name: _____

Ending

98. Hot Air Balloon

. . . but we never thought it was a hot air balloon!" I told the balloonist.

"Yes, they sound much louder than people think," she said. "It's even scarier if you're caught off guard!"

By now, lots of our neighbors had come out to the street to see what all the fuss was about. In a small town like ours, it's not every day you see what we just saw.

Soon a flatbed truck pulled onto our street.

"That's my ride home," the balloonist said. "My team followed me on the ground."

"They can fit this huge balloon in that little truck?" my friend Meredith asked.

"It has to be folded first. Do you guys want to help me pack up the balloon?"

"We'd love to!" I said.

Name: _____

Starter

99. Meteorite

I remember learning in science class that meteors often burn up after entering Earth's atmosphere. One that doesn't completely vaporize and hits the ground is called a meteorite.

"I'd love to see a meteorite land!" I said.

"Good luck," my friend Jay said. "I would, too, but you can't predict when or where they'll land. And I'm not waiting around for a space rock to bonk me on the head."

That was a year ago. Last night, as my family drove home from a restaurant, the last thing I was thinking about was meteorites. As we were about to pull into the driveway, something streaked across the sky and thumped onto the pavement right in front of us. My mom braked the car just in time.

"Don't move," she said. She turned the high beams on to see better, and when she did we all . . .

Name: _____

Landed on Your Street

Ending

100. Injured Bird

". . . you did the right thing to call us," the woman said. She said a lot of birds get hurt every day, but a lot of people don't know that they can call an animal protection office like hers for help.

My brother and I watched her carefully lift the little bird with special gloves and put him in a box with air holes and water.

"We named him already," I said. "When we saw him get hurt, I felt sad, but he seemed strong—like a little Hercules. So we called him Hercules."

"I'm sure Hercules will be very happy when you come visit him at the animal hospital," she said.

My brother said, "And soon, he'll back on his feet—uh, wings—again!"

Name: _____

Landed on Your Street

Starter

101. Book of Spells

"Do you think it's real?" my friend Harris asked.

"I don't know," I said. "I've never seen a book of spells before, real or fake."

"I've never seen any book in the middle of the road," Harris said.

"That's why it probably is a book of spells," I said. "Maybe a witch dropped it while she was flying on her broomstick."

"Spells and witches? You don't believe in all that, do you?" Harris said.

"Well, a book of spells wouldn't exist if there were no witches, right?"

We opened the book. Harris said, "I don't think it's in a weird language. I think this is French or German, maybe."

"Let's test it. I'll say one of these sentences and we'll see what happens," I said.

"I don't know if that's a good idea," Harris said nervously.

"I thought you didn't believe it was a book of spells," I said, smiling. Then I read the first sentence out loud and . . .

One-Sentence Starters

102. My first day at the new school went fine, but my sister can't say the same.

103. Ed knew exactly where to go; he just didn't know how to get there.

104. Not everyone has an elf living in his closet, but my best friend does.

105. My alarm rang at 3 A.M.—five hours earlier than I set it for.

106. I went to sleep in New York and woke up in London.

107. Ray saw something shiny in the sand up ahead.

108. "Tell me a story about when you were a little kid," I asked the President of the United States.

109. When I came home, I found my neighbors in our house and my parents in theirs.

110. "That's weird," Caroline said, "I had the exact same dream last night."

111. It's been one year since I gave up eating chocolate.

112. Three words were written on the blackboard—and they made us all groan.

113. When I opened my e-mail, the first words I saw were, "You have 403 new messages."

114. The phone rang and someone knocked on the door at the same time.

115. We weren't having a blackout, yet none of the electrical devices in our house worked.

116. "When I was your age, I almost became a movie star," grandpa said.

117. I saw someone in the store that looked just like my best friend from kindergarten.

118. I knew the zoo's rule: "Don't feed the animals," and I wish I had respected it.

119. For my mom's birthday, I decided to make her breakfast in bed.

120. The group of weary travelers stepped onto the shore of the strange, new land.

121. Joel practiced guitar every day after school, but not because he wanted to be a rock star.

122. My best friend and I decided that we'd trade places for a day.

123. I don't believe in ghosts, aliens, or fairies, but I do believe in monsters.

124. As my mom took the old painting off the wall, a dusty envelope that had been hidden behind it fell to the floor.

125. Jake searched his room to find things he could donate to charity.

126. "Originally, you weren't going to be named Laura," my mom said.

127. Tonight I found out that my cousin Kevin isn't really my cousin at all.

128. The dog ran up to the biggest tree in the area and began barking.

129. "Five of you will stay here, and four of you will come with me," the leader said.

130. I opened my eyes and saw about ten fireflies in my bedroom!

131. Dan lit a candle and said, "I think we're all going to be here for a while."

132. Diana looked up "human" in the dictionary and was shocked when she couldn't find the word there.

133. Lucy was acting weird all day long, much weirder than cats usually do.

134. Tyler looked at the obstacle course with fear in his eyes.

135. "Raise your hand if you're ready for this test," our teacher said.

136. "I've been to every state but one," Tawana said, "and I'll never go there."

137. We found the perfect spot for our picnic—that is, until we realized we were trespassing.

138. Mitch had to deliver the letter before sunset, but the gate was locked.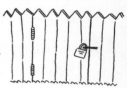

139. Just as my dad was about to light a fire, something flew down the chimney and into the family room.

140. Ever since I ate that apple, I haven't been able to stop sneezing.

One-Sentence Endings

141. Luckily, the rain didn't come until the whole thing was over.

142. Only two of us had gone in, but three of us came out.

143. "I told you it wouldn't work no matter what you tried," Rick said.

144. "The second and third wishes worked out great, but I wish I could take back my first wish," Darlia said to the genie.

145. As they cracked the door open nervously, they discovered the room was empty except for one red marble.

146. When Meg got home, the bike she thought was stolen was lying on the lawn.

147. Amelia promised herself that she would always bring a camera with her from now on.

148. As she walked up the driveway, the smell of baking cookies filled the air.

149. For the first time all day, everyone smiled—even me.

150. After that, Jack said he was through accepting dares.

151. It was the second-best vacation I've ever had.

152. Sixty people showed up, and every one of them was named "Paul."

153. There was a time when my dad would have thought it was funny, but not anymore.

154. This just proves that ordering a pizza is not always as easy as it's supposed to be.

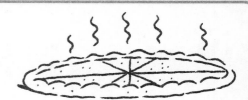

155. "We'd better play a different game next time," Isabella said.

156. Thirty seconds after he left, the doorbell rang.

157. I suddenly noticed why—I was wearing two different shoes.

158. "I better go take a bath," Grace said with a giggle.

159. The whole family went around the neighborhood to take down the "Lost Dog" flyers together.

160. Steve looked me straight in the eye and said, "My real name is Gordon."

161. This time, the footprints in the snow were going away from the house.

162. We only got three hours of sleep that night.

163. After rereading the e-mail about ten times, I took a deep breath and clicked on "Send."

164. We decided we'd had enough of the future and reset the time machine to visit the past.

165. The race proved who was faster, but it proved something else as well.

166. "That's why I didn't tell you the truth from the beginning," Ms. Sloane said.

167. It was the only blizzard she'd ever experienced.

168. In the morning, I not only felt like a whole new person, I literally was a new person.

169. "April Fool's—one day early," said Martin.

170. We decided to paint the tree house again—but this time, any other color besides red.

171. Then we understood why our teacher had been so grumpy all week.

172. "I've changed my mind," Alina said. "I think I'd rather be an pilot instead."

173. When my parents weren't looking, the waiter winked at me and I winked back.

174. Everyone agreed that we would find a new campsite next year.

175. She left before I got the chance to thank her.

176. Gerard almost caught it, but it escaped at the last second.

177. That's why we named him "Whisper."

178. I grew two inches since this started.

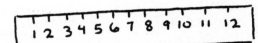

179. When the smell of burnt toast came from the kitchen, I knew everything was back to normal.

180. "This is so much better than the gift you gave me last year," grandma said.